Fact Finders™

Questions and Answers: Physical Science

Electricity

A Question and Answer Book

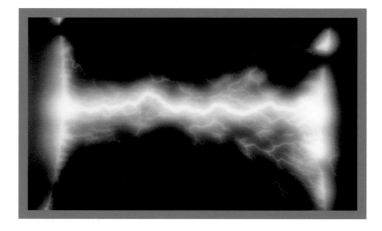

by Adele Richardson

Consultant:
Philip W. Hammer, PhD
Vice President, The Franklin Center
The Franklin Institute Science Museum
Philadelphia, Pennsylvania

Capstone
press
Mankato, Minnesota

Fact Finders is published by Capstone Press,
151 Good Counsel Drive, P.O. Box 669, Mankato, Minnesota 56002.
www.capstonepress.com

Library of Congress Cataloging-in-Publication Data
Richardson, Adele, 1966–
    Electricity: a question and answer book / by Adele Richardson.
    p. cm.—(Fact finders. Questions and answers. Physical science)
    Summary: "Introduces electricity and its generation, components, movement, and
functions in a question and answer format"—Provided by publisher.
    Includes bibliographical references and index.
    ISBN-13: 978-0-7368-5444-3 (hardcover)
    ISBN-10: 0-7368-5444-4 (hardcover)
    1. Electricity—Juvenile literature. I. Title. II. Series.
QC527.2.R53 2006
537—dc22   2005020117

Editorial Credits
Chris Harbo editor; Juliette Peters, designer; Tami Collins, illustrator; Jo Miller, photo researcher;
    Scott Thoms, photo editor

Photo Credits
Capstone Press/Karon Dubke, 4, 7, 12, 19, 20, 21, 22, 27, 29 (all)
Corbis, Bettmann, 6; Lester Lefkowitz, 8; Roger Ressmeyer, 14
Digital Stock, 24
Fundamental Photographs/Jeff J. Daly, 15
Getty Images Inc./Stone/Geopress, 13
Library of Congress, 25
Photo Researchers Inc./P. Jude, 1; Science Photo Library/Steve Allen, cover
Seapics.com, 26
Visuals Unlimited/David Wrobel, 23

1 2 3 4 5 6 11 10 09 08 07 06

Table of Contents

Features

What is electricity?

An alarm clock rings in the bedroom.
In the kitchen, an overhead light blinks on.
Open the refrigerator and the milk is cold.
What do all these things have in common?
They all happen because of electricity.

Without electricity you might find it hard to get up in time for school.

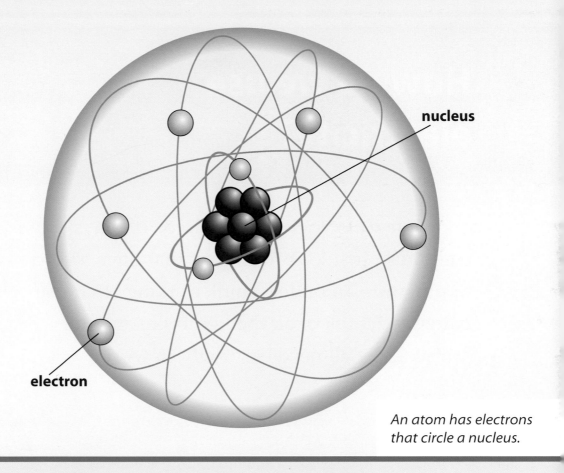

nucleus

electron

An atom has electrons that circle a nucleus.

But what is electricity? It's a kind of energy related to the **atom**. Atoms are tiny particles that we can't see. They make up everything in the universe. In the center of each atom is a **nucleus** made of smaller particles. Circling around the nucleus are **electrons**. Electricity is made when electrons move from one atom to another.

How do we use electricity?

We use electricity in hundreds of ways every day. Just look for things that have a cord to plug into an outlet. Think of things that use batteries. Think of all the lightbulbs in your house. They all need electricity to work.

Fact!

Thomas Edison invented the first long-lasting lightbulb in 1879.

A toaster uses electricity to turn frozen waffles into a hot breakfast.

Electricity brings to life many of the sights and sounds that fill our days. Computers, TVs, and handheld video games would be nothing but blank screens without electricity. And stereos, smoke alarms, and doorbells fall silent when the power goes out. Try making toast or waffles for breakfast. Chances are, you'll need electricity.

How is electricity made?

Most of the electricity we use is made at power plants. Power plants all over the country make electricity night and day, all year long. Most of these plants burn coal, oil, or natural gas to boil water. Why? Because boiling water creates steam that turns the blades on a machine called a **turbine**.

A coal-burning power plant uses tons of coal to make electricity.

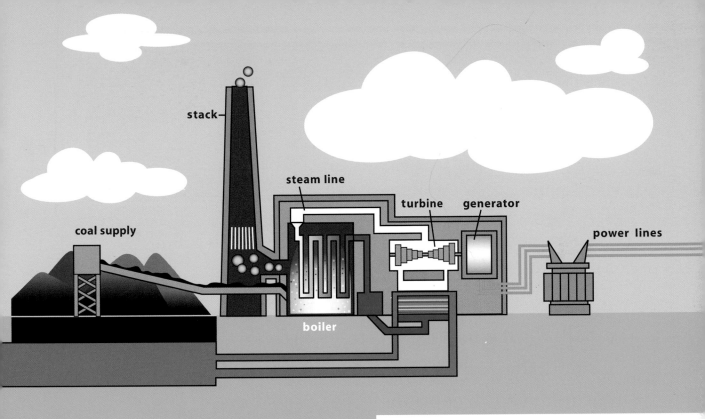

stack

steam line

turbine   generator

coal supply

power lines

boiler

Burning coal heats water in a power plant's boiler. Steam from the water turns the turbine connected to the electric generator.

Turbines have blades that spin around like a windmill. The blades are connected to one end of a long shaft. The other end of the shaft is connected to a **generator**. When the turbine blades spin, the generator makes electricity.

What is an electric current?

An electric **current** is a flow of electricity. How does it work? First, a current needs moving electrons. Second, a current needs a path for the moving electrons to follow. Usually the path is a wire. Lastly, an electric current needs a constant force to push the electrons along the path.

Fact!

Stay away from power lines! The electric current in a power line is strong enough to stop your heart. Every year, people die by accidentally touching power lines while working outdoors.

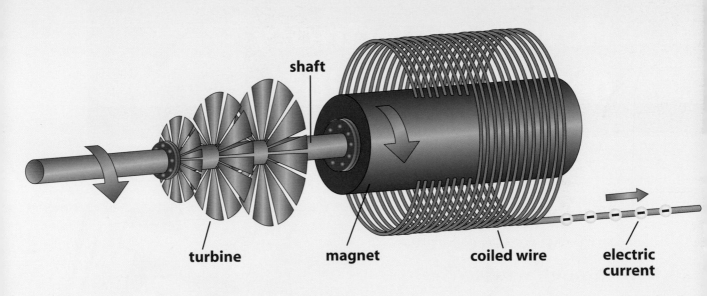

shaft

turbine　　　　**magnet**　　　　**coiled wire**　　　**electric current**

A generator uses a spinning magnet to create an electric current in a coiled wire.

A power plant uses a generator to create an electric current. A spinning magnet inside the generator pushes electrons from atom to atom along a coiled wire. As long as the magnet spins, the electrons have a constant force that keeps them moving. If the magnet stops, the current is broken—lights out!

How does electricity get to a lightbulb?

Electricity travels to lightbulbs, TVs, and microwave ovens through wires. Why wires? Because wire is a great **conductor**. Anything that electricity can flow through is called a conductor. Metals like steel, iron, and copper conduct electricity really well. Most electrical wires are made of copper.

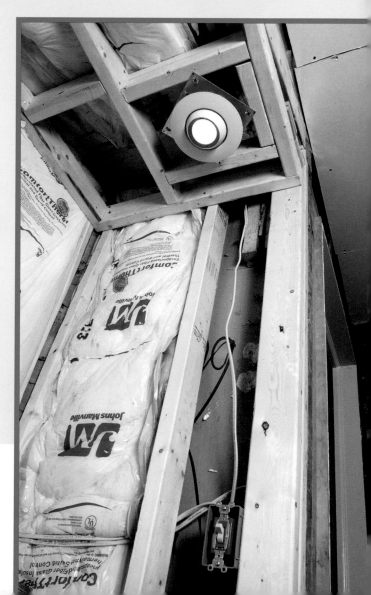

Electricity travels to lights through wires in the wall.

Power cables are strung up on poles or buried underground.

But how did the electricity get to your house in the first place? It traveled through a cable. On the outside, a cable looks like a thick rope. Inside, the cable has a cluster of wires. These wires conduct electricity from the power plant to a central power box in your home. From there, wires bring electricity to all the rooms of your house.

Why do electricians wear rubber gloves?

Electricians wear rubber gloves to protect themselves. If they didn't, they could get **electrocuted**. The rubber in the gloves is an **insulator**. An insulator is anything that electricity does not flow through. Wood, glass, and cotton are other insulators.

Rubber gloves protect a utility worker from getting a shock while working on a power line.

O VOLT

Plastic covers wires that carry electricity through our homes.

We rely on insulators every day. The cords of lamps, hair dryers, and computers are all covered with a plastic coating. The plastic is an insulator. It stops the current from shocking our bodies or starting fires. Electricity can be very dangerous. Remember, never use anything electrical if wires are poking through the insulator.

How do batteries make electricity?

Batteries are like little portable power plants. They allow us to use electricity without having cords plugged into the wall. Things like cars, cellular phones, and toys all use batteries.

Fact!

In 1888, German scientist Carl Gassner invented the first "dry" cell battery. This battery was very much like the alkaline batteries we use today.

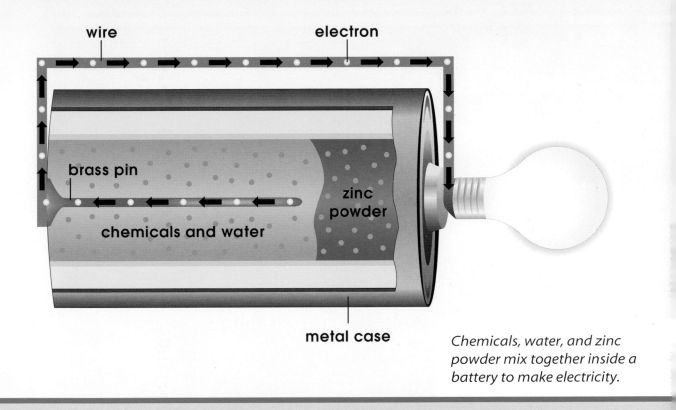

wire　　　　electron

brass pin

chemicals and water

zinc
powder

metal case

Chemicals, water, and zinc powder mix together inside a battery to make electricity.

Alkaline batteries are often used in radios and flashlights. On the outside, these batteries have a metal case with a plastic coating. Inside are chemicals and water that mix with zinc powder to make a paste. The paste touches the brass pin in the center of the battery. Contact between the pin and the paste loosens up electrons so they can move. When conductors are attached to both ends of a battery, an electric current flows.

How does a flashlight work?

A flashlight works because it has a **circuit**. In fact, everything that uses electricity has a circuit. A circuit is a looping path that electric current follows. A flashlight's circuit has a lightbulb, metal conductors, a switch, and batteries. These four parts connect together to form the circuit's loop.

Fact!

The wiring in all new homes is connected to a circuit breaker. It breaks a circuit when an electric current in a wire rises so high it could start a fire.

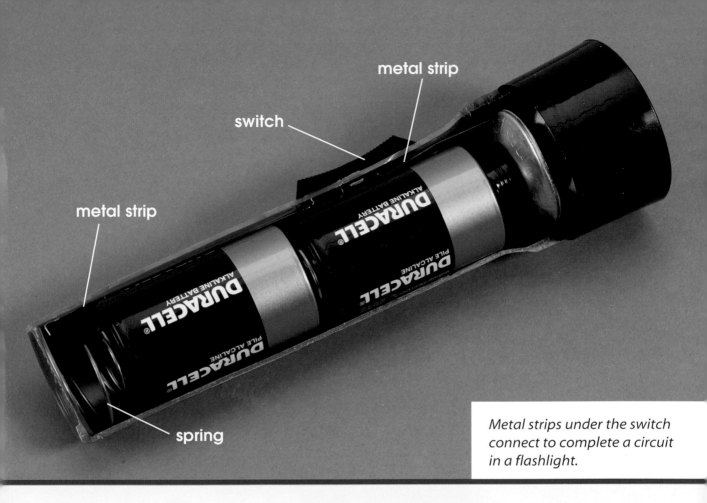

metal strip

switch

metal strip

spring

Metal strips under the switch connect to complete a circuit in a flashlight.

In a flashlight, a spring and thin strips of metal conduct electrons from the batteries. Turning the flashlight's switch on causes the metal strips to touch. The circuit becomes closed and electricity flows to the lightbulb. Then electrons flow into the end of a battery marked with a plus sign. As long as the switch is on, electricity travels around the loop.

Why do I sometimes get a shock when I touch someone?

The shock you feel is from static electricity. Static electricity builds up and stays in one place. It doesn't keep moving like electricity does for a lightbulb. Static electricity is at rest until it comes in contact with an object. Or another person.

Yow! That hurt! Static electricity can give you quite a shock.

Rubbing your feet on carpet causes electrons to move from the carpet to your body.

Moving electrons play a part in static electricity. Carpet has atoms with electrons whirling around them. When your feet touch carpet, some electrons move onto your body. Sometimes when you touch another person, the electrons jump from your hand. You feel a shock as the electrons move from you to the other person.

Why do we measure electricity?

We measure electricity so we know how much energy something needs. Take a look at an unlit lightbulb. A bulb marked 100W means that it needs 100 **watts** of power to work. If it gets less, the bulb won't glow as brightly. Most things that use electricity are marked with watts. The higher the number of watts, the more energy it needs to work.

A 100 watt lightbulb uses more energy and puts out more light than a 60 watt bulb.

Electric meters have several dials to help measure the amount of electricity homes use every month.

The power company measures the electricity we use. Every month, they read meters at our homes and schools. The meters keep track of the electricity we use. We pay the power company for making the electricity.

Why did Benjamin Franklin fly a kite in a storm?

More than 250 years ago, Benjamin Franklin was fascinated by electricity. He studied experiments that other scientists of his time were doing. As he did his own tests with electricity, he became curious about lightning. Was it electricity made by nature?

Franklin tested his idea. He tied a wire to a kite and a metal key to the kite's string. In June 1752, he flew the kite on a stormy night.

Fact!

Lightning is really a super strong form of static electricity. Lightning is made in clouds when wind rubs tiny pieces of ice together.

Franklin knew lightning was electricity when he saw how it traveled down the wire and wet string to the key.

Suddenly, lightning struck! It traveled down the wire and wet string to the key. Sparks shot out. When Franklin saw how the lightning traveled, he was certain that it was a form of electricity.

Do I have electricity in me?

Your body sure does! It depends on electricity to work right. Electric signals travel along **nerves** in your body. Nerves act like wires. They let your body send messages to your spinal cord and brain. In return, your brain and spinal cord send messages back to your body.

Fact!

A fish called the electric ray can create electricity inside its body. It shocks other fish to stun them before it eats them.

Nerves in your hand send electric signals to your spinal cord. If you touch a hot cup, your spinal cord makes you pull your hand away.

These messages can help keep you from getting hurt. When you touch a cup, electric signals travel along nerves to your spinal cord. If the cup is hot, your spinal cord causes a reaction that makes you pull your hand away.

Fast Facts about Electricity

- Electricity is created when electrons travel from one atom to another.

- Electrons flow in an electric current only if they have a place to go, such as around a circuit.

- A circuit is a looping path that electricity follows.

- Conductors are materials that allow electricity to pass through them. Metals, such as copper, iron, and steel, are excellent conductors.

- Insulators are materials that don't allow electricity to pass through them easily. Rubber, wood, and plastic are good insulators.

- Switches turn electric currents on and off by opening or closing the circuit.

- A battery is also called a cell.

- Nerve cells in your body carry electric signals to your brain.

Hands On: Build a Circuit

Everything that runs on electricity uses a circuit. Ask an adult to help you with this activity to see how a circuit works.

What You Need

masking tape
2 pieces of copper wire, 6 inches (15 centimeters) long
D-size battery
table
flashlight bulb

What You Do

1. *Tape the end of one wire to the end of the battery marked with the plus sign.*
2. *Tape the end of the other wire to the end of the battery marked with the minus sign.*
3. *Lay your battery and wires on the table in front of you. Bend the loose ends of the wires toward each other to form a rough circle. Do not let the wires touch each other because they may get hot.*
4. *Lay the flashlight bulb on the table between the loose ends of the wires.*
5. *Press the end of the wire from the minus end of the battery to the side of the metal casing below the bulb.*
6. *Touch the end of the wire from the plus end of the battery to the metal bump at the bottom of the bulb. Watch what happens.*

Did your bulb light up? When both wires touched the bulb, you created a closed circuit. Electricity was able to flow from the battery to the bulb and back to the battery. What happens when you take one wire off the bulb? Doing so creates an open circuit. Does your bulb stay lit?

29

Glossary

atom (AT-uhm)—an element in its smallest form

circuit (SUR-kit)—a path for electricity to flow through

conductor (kuhn-DUHK-tur)—a material that lets electricity, heat, or sound travel easily through it; metal is a good conductor of electricity.

current (KUR-uhnt)—a flow of electric charge

electrocute (i-LEK-truh-kyoot)—to injure or kill with a severe electric shock

electron (i-LEK-tron)—a tiny particle in an atom that travels around the nucleus; electrons carry a negative charge.

generator (JEN-uh-ray-tur)—a machine that makes electricity by turning a magnet inside a coil of wire

insulator (IN-suh-lay-tur)—a material that blocks an electrical current

nerve (NURV)—a bundle of thin fibers that sends messages between your brain and other parts of your body

nucleus (NOO-klee-uhss)—the center of an atom; the nucleus is made up of protons and neutrons.

turbine (TUR-bine)—a set of blades that turn a magnet in a generator to make electricity

watt (WOT)—a unit for measuring electrical power

Internet Sites

FactHound offers a safe, fun way to find Internet sites related to this book. All of the sites on FactHound have been researched by our staff.

Here's how:
1. Visit *www.facthound.com*
2. Type in this special code **0736854444** for age-appropriate sites. Or enter a search word related to this book for a more general search.
3. Click on the **Fetch It** button.

FactHound will fetch the best sites for you!

Read More

Cooper, Christopher. *Electricity: From Amps to Volts.* Science Answers. Chicago: Heinemann, 2004.

Hunter, Rebecca. *The Facts about Electricity.* Science, the Facts. North Mankato, Minn.: Smart Apple Media, 2005.

Llewellyn, Claire. *Electricity.* Start-up Science. North Mankato, Minn: Cherrytree, 2005.

Stille, Darlene R. *Electricity.* Science Around Us. Chanhassen, Minn.: Child's World, 2005.

Index

11/14/06